REVEALED

THE BOOK OF REVELATION (BOOK 3 of 3)

Revealed, Introduction

BOOK 1

DARKNESS

Night

Humans

Sex

Destiny

The Enemy

Religion

Masquerade

Struggle

Pain

Death

BOOK 2

REVELATION

Deliverance

The First Day of My Life

Truth

Spirit

Blood

Prayer

Sign

Love

Gift & Talent

Grace

BOOK 3

LIGHT

Day

Life

Time

Faith

Freedom

Money

Happiness

Angel

Sign

Imperfection & Grace

Revealed

WHAT'S GOING ON

You can go to church every Sunday for thirty years and listen to best celebrity pastors in the world, you can kneel at the finest altars around the world ,you read every book about spirituality and consciousness, the force of life and how it merges with your personality and power of attraction, you earn a nine PhD's from Harvard and own all the precious stones in the world but your life will not be complete until your blessed with the true revelation of your life. Billions of us live our lives from generation to generation without ever experiencing the power of true revelation. The hidden things of the world are revealed to a chosen few amongst us. Philippians 3:10 " That I may know you and the power behind your resurrection" this was the desperation that Paul had to have a deep revelation of God and life.

Why are the Kennedy's dying? Why are the Getty's cursed, Why cant money buy you happiness, good health and life without sorrow and pain? Week after week, you turn on the news and hear of an NFL player who kills himself and loses a hundred million dollar in a few bad deals, you hear a beautiful actress who can't find happiness after a dozen relationships with the most handsome men in the world.

Why did that beautiful young songstress die so young? Why do reformed drug addicts relapse a thousand times over, you can add a thousand questions of your own but here's the kicker, there's only one answer. The answer to all these questions is that we live in a world where the majority of us can only see the physical things around us; we make all our decisions about the most things of our life based on half the information. The other half is unseen, unrevealed, silent, but very alive. They have eyes but can't see, they have ears but don't hear, and they are destroyed from lack of wisdom. Hosea 4:6 "My people are destroyed from lack of knowledge ". The word "from" means it's not a one day or one time thing, but a continuous ignorance that leads to death and destruction.

From the time of creation, man was first a spirit according to Genesis 1:26 ". Then God said, let us make man in our image, after our likeness, "If we are the image of God then we are spirit living in a body just as he is, so we are. 1 John 1:17.

Revealed is a concept book that powerfully shifts the paradigm in the understanding of our human life here in the physical realm and the forces that affect the outcome, quality and purpose of our individual existence. The knowledge that is contained in this material, if understood with the context that its written, will change your life for the best. Life is rich, beautiful, exciting and amazingly fulfilling if you understand, nurture and appreciate the fundamental principles that shape it (Christ). Conversely, life can be hell on earth, even for the richest and most successful amongst us, if they live in denial or ignorance of the subjects that are humbly defined herein. Hard hitting and thought provoking as it might seem, this work is inspired through the divine grace of the Holy Spirit through which all darkness is made light, all pain is remedied, all dreams are fulfilled and truth endures. John 14:6 I am the way the truth and the life

This piece is written in three parts. The first section is Darkness, a state of being blind or lost. The second section is Revelation, which deals with the awakening of the truth and the final part is Light. This section focuses on how to live in the aftermath of a great revelation. As you take this journey amidst an aesthetic collection of thematic images and life changing thoughts, we urge you to share your new comprehension and confidence in the knowledge of the unseen and the unknown. Start the conversation, and join us online to grow and apply yourself, capture the moment and seize this opportunity to be guided by God's grace. It is not our intention to lead you astray or cause you to question your religion or faith but we challenge you to seek the simple truth and open your eyes to the reality of your life. Depending on the power positive thinking, the laws of attraction or hoping that the constellation of the stars will change your life is absurd and sad to say the least. By the help of the Holy Spirit and dedication to the Holy bible I received the Gift of Revelation in these teachings that gave me a heartbeat to the ideas and subjects covered in this book.

This creation is truly inspired by her patience, determination and insa tiable appetite to stand and lead with the truth. Some of her sayings might remind you of the scriptures but in the final analysis, it's about life, and the tools we all need to live it well, in spite of our various religions and beliefs.

In the face of constant departure from the truth, pointless pain and struggle, our inability to understand the unknown or to find the meaning to our lives, we end up in the hopeless pursuit of happiness without ever fully experiencing the fulfillment it should bring into our lives.

LIGHT

Now that you have come into light from the dark, do take a moment to be thankful for all that has been revealed to you, for it is all by grace. Many will walk this earth and not see, hear, touch, feel nor experience the power of God's Revelation. When you come into the light, you see all there is, you start to live armed with the right amount of information you should always have. Stand tall and walk in the light and beware of forces that wish to relegate you to your past. Free yourself from the darkness of your infancy and begin to explore the true meaning and purpose of your life by mastering the following concepts. Mathew 5:14-16.

DAY

To see the daylight every day is a blessing and we must remain thankful to awake from the dead of night into it. For every billion people that went to sleep, they're thousands that never awoke to see the light of day. Rom 9:16. We have the gift of day to seize time and accomplish that which we have set out to do.

One must not underestimate the power of one day because your life can change during the events of one single day. The day represents a huge segment of the physical realm of our life because we see things come into being without any thought of what's behind it. In the same way, the night represents some of the spiritual aspects of our life because during the night, our physical being is transported, through the inevitable act of sleep, into a realm where our physical form has no use. We enter the night, dead to the long day past and in it we experience a shadow of what is to come during the *Day* of our lives. To truly seize the day, you must arrest the night before and align yourself with the maker of all things to insure and ensure the positive outcomes of your day. Romans 13:11,12. In the book of Job, the Lord asked Job, have you commanded your morning to give you it's harvest?

LIFE

To have and understand the true gift of life, the gift of good health through the grace of God is the culmination of our first step to wisdom. It's our duty to protect the life that we've been given. John 10:10. When we lose respect for life, we disrespect the essence of God's human manifestation, the entire creation of our existence, and the universe that houses it. With all that we have accomplished through the advancement of science, evolution and the history and origin of the living, Life is the one thing that's unequivocally given and taken by God. No one has any jurisdiction over how we get here and how we leave. When our life form ceases to have its breath, all that remains is memories, deeds and legacies for the lucky ones. What will you give back for the gift of life God has given you? Romans 6:1. Shall we remain in sin that grace may abound? God forbid.

TIME

Time is one thing we cannot control, but we can control what we do with our time. We have the choice of shaping time to serve us and it's easy to assume that we have all the time in the world, Mathew 25:13. However what's important about the concept of time is to realize that our schedule is not God's schedule Mathew 24:36. We may decide to put direct effort into achieving a goal, a dream, an ideal or a specific milestone with a set time in mind. Oftentimes we end up with less than satisfactory results because we depend on human factors to guarantee our achievements. God has a perfect time for us to reach our goal because he sees beyond our human and physical timelines. Sometimes he stalls in order to save our lives. Therefore, we must exercise an acceptance of his time for us, remain focused on the path and the human tasks we must carry out knowing that in due time we will reach that goal. As we wait for God's time, our impatience is expected and sometimes we seek a faster option, which ultimately becomes a thorn.

FAITH

The tragedy is that faith is probably the most powerful but underutilized force in the natural world. We know what it is, we certainly understand it but many fail to remember and apply it. You often hear people say that if you can dream it, then you can achieve it. We also know that faith without works means nothing and as well work without faith is dead James 2:14-26. Therefore, there's a conditional correlation between faith and work. Sometimes the intensity of work you put into a project or an endeavor not only makes it a success, but it may inspire great faith in others. In other words, faith is transferable and when you successfully experience it once, it becomes unimaginable to move forward with it.

Every step we take into the unknown should be guided by faith because that first leap is always scary. Some people operate with blind faith but the most powerful faith experience one can have, in my experience, come from having a personal communication with God about something you need. Romans 4:22; When you lay out your needs in the presence of your creator, a faith-fueled conversation is established. Isaiah 43:26; come let us reason together "However faith will fail you if you don't believe in yourself. The prerequisite to engaging the power of faith is finding that, within us lies the amazing authority to trust the tangible realization of that dream. Faith is the strength to believe in things presently unseen but felt and experienced within you as though it were there. One must develop that muscle to sustain faith. A pastor gave a prophecy to a man about the name of his church which meant confinement and yet he was believing God for thousands of members, lesson: your faith must show in your actions and words. Hebrew 11:6, for without faith it is impossible to please the lord.

FREEDOM

America is sometimes referred as the land of the free, yet we have highest population of incarcerated people of any industrialized nation in the world. We have U.S troops dying around the world every day, to protect and maintain the quality of a life we have as a free nation. On a personal level, how should we define freedom? I contend that freedom is a basic human need but it seems like the more you desire it, the less you have and the less you need, the more freedom you have. For instance, we now live in an era of high technology that's supposed to make our lives easier and more efficient, but because we depend on it so much, access to every aspect of our lives are constantly monitored, reviewed and stored away, thus taking away every ounce of our freedom. Ironically freedom has now become the price we have to pay for the freedom of expressing ourselves. The U.S financial collapse of 2007 made us realize how much of our financial freedom can be taken away when our mortgages, high-interest rates and personal debt don't play out well in the open market. Our credit card debts enslave us every day and yet we fail to understand it.

From a spiritual perspective, many of us are in complete bondage, unaware of how strapped down we are to our addictions, idolatry, generational curses, the hateful envy of friends, the pain of family relationships and the hopelessness of broken dreams. The most valuable *free-dom* is knowing how much God plays a part in ensuring our peaceful freedom in everyday living. 2 Corinthians 3:17.

MONEY

Money, Power and Respect tend to work hand in hand but money usually takes precedence. The most common saying about money is that *"the love of money is the root of all evil"*. 1 Tim 6:10, time, money and now information, is probably the new currency of our generation, which essentially constitutes wealth. By simple definition, money is the preferred medium of exchange for goods and services rendered, but the lack of money raises several questions in our lives. To understand the true concept of money, one must be fully accountable for their time and money. Furthermore, because money plays such a vital role in our lives, various frames of references have been developed over thousands of years to help us comprehend its meaning. Here are a few of those thoughts- when you're not making money, there's a great chance that you're probably spending it. When you spend more than you make, it's hard to emancipate yourself from the enslavement of debt. Discipline and accountability or lack thereof, tends to be the compass by which we can interpret the meaning of money and its effects on our lives. Notable speakers on the subject of money, specifically Jim Rohn, contends that "we don't get paid for the hours spent on our jobs, but instead for the value we bring to the company in those hours." This why the Ceo at Disney makes $52,000,000 a year, while the security guards brings $23,000 for the same amount of time. In our world today, you get paid for your value and there's no common ground or hard and fast rules.

Different rules apply to different types of money, fast drug money is fleeting, hard earned money sticks around, some people are born into money while other emerge from a life complete poverty to tremendous wealth and prestige. From a spiritual school of thought, everyone, from our inception, is afforded a means of making money and creating a better life, but oftentimes *life's obstacles* get in the way of those possibilities and blessings.

Some obstacles are physical, while others are non-physical and most people only look at the surface issues without having any clue. In fact, majority of our fights are spiritual fights against principalities and powers of darkness in high places, Ephesians 6:12. On a physical level, we can blame factors such as the economy, character, employment, level of education and skill, location and industry, but the story doesn't end there. When under an evil influence, you might make several errors in judgment that causes you lose to a big investment deal, a home, perhaps divorce or just trusting in enemies posing like friends. By questioning specific situations is your life concerning your income with respect to the hard work you in put it, you'll become more aware of evil interferences in your financial homestead. If the numbers don't add up or match the labor your putting in, then something is wrong, indeed several things might be wrong. When you can't come to grips with how fast money escapes your life without having something to show for it, then it's time to seek the help of someone who's gifted with the power of revelation eg. prophets, pastors or even elders for counseling.

HAPPINESS

The pursuit of happiness is at the core of everything we desire. It is actually a fruit of the spirit, Galatians 2:22. This ideal state is one that we've tried to understand over the ages. Here are what we know-Money can't buy you happiness, success may not fulfill your heart's desire and nothing we do can guarantee absolute happiness. Hence it's my belief that true happiness is a gift from God as stated above. They're people amongst us who are always happy in spite of their hopeless conditions, financial instability, broken dreams and endless suffering. Still they smile and have a natural and effortless appreciation for life, joy, love and happiness. Furthermore, the happiness they feel is engraved in their hearts and no matter how hard you try, you can't take this joy away from them because is from the lord. Happiness when seen, is an external expression of the gift of joy feeling felt inside and this is why trying to find bliss externally never works. We shop until the malls close, some resort to hard drugs, alcohol and hedonism but the temporary high you get from external things soon wear off and you're left with an emptier heart and a wider void in your soul. Seek therefore the source of spiritual happiness that's found in God's own gift of his Love. Some of the happiest people in the world have nothing. Having talked about the good side of happiness, it's important that we look at the other side of the coin, sadness. Depression and sadness are dominant evil forces that could take over your life and cause you to hate everything around you. It robs you of your function as a human being and in its extreme form, it may lead to suicidal thoughts. This tormenting spirit is hardly noticeable on a smiling face, because its host may be very successful and in complete control of their life. Sometimes our amazing success may blind us from seeing the truth, but when you're alone with all your diamonds, hedge funds and private jets and still can't find true happiness, you'll know what really matters in life. Happiness is vital part of our life because it motivates, inspires us to live, grow, create, love and share. To find true happiness, look inside yourself and start a conversation with God about his purpose for your life. When this question is asked with sincerity, it opens a doorway to light, your reason for living. Having the freedom to do what you love, with the gifts that you've been given will fulfill your heart and raise to a higher dimension of happiness, but always ask the Lord to give you the kind of happiness that comes from he's eternal peace and constant grace. This is the form of happiness that's contagious because it comes from God's love for you, and it's so much bigger than the joy of fulfillment you'll get from accomplishing your earthly goals. It helps and makes destiny fulfillment easier as said in Isaiah 12:3.

ANGEL

In the end, we are not alone because God will always send you an Angel, someone who enters your live at the right time, for the right purpose, without explanation or rationale. Angels amongst us are always trying to enter our hearts but most people don't see them. Sometimes we recognize their presence but feel too lazy to embrace their message, Gen 32:22-31. When God cares about you, he'll send you angels at the various key point in your life, to stir you to the right path when you go astray. Many people live their lives without experiencing the guidance and protection that comes when *he* sends his angels before you. Psalm 91:11-12. Some unseen angels are deployed to watch over you every moment of your life and although most of us can't see them, it pays to thank them daily. We've all heard stories of fatal car crashes where all but one person survived or the story about a friend that missed a flight that crashed a few hours later. God is with us all the time because he knows that we keep making the wrong turn, for one second, can end your life. We get insurance to protect us before an accident occurs, but when you entrust your life in God, who knows the future dates of all your lives incidents, what then should your premium be? Priceless. All we have to give is gratitude and appreciation because we don't have enough *thanks* to give the army of angels that watch over us every second of our lives.

SIGN

A sign is probably the simplest and most direct evidence of God's will
in our lives. He will give you a sign, sometimes its light and airy and
other times its hard hitting and resounding. These signs are given to
you to define his true position with respect to serious matters in your
life. For example, you could be in what appears to be a loving relationship on the surface, but because your maker knows that this same relationship might cost you your life, he orchestrates an event or sets of
circumstances that causes you to leave that relationship. There's a very
thin line between those that recognize these subtle signs and those that
don't, or fail to act on it. As you grow spiritually aware and stronger,
every cell in your physical body reacts to any foreign presence in your
spiritual landscape, thus making you more prepared to defend or attack
negative forces. On a lighter note, some signs are like smiling miracles
that happen to you during the course of your day. It might be as simple
as getting a very good bargain on a shoe you've always wanted
or through your dream or a delightful and personal experience that you
know clearly must be from God, as a sign that he's still with you.

IMPERFECTION

There's no perfection is mankind that's why we live in pursuit of it. Mark 10:18. Only God is perfect and this is supposed to be a very simple concept to come to terms with but it escapes us in our day-to-day lives. From the stand point of sin, experience will teach you that although your spirit is willing to be righteous and you fight to stay faithful, often times you'll fall from grace. After a few falls with hopeless regret, you might eventually come to the simple realization that one cannot completely live in perfection, free from all sin but yet striving for righteousness through grace. This understanding is the birthing of wisdom because it allows you the nobility of surrendering to the most high, the one who know no flaws, the Alfa and Omega through whom, everything is made perfect. There's a new kind of realignment that happens to you when you walk with the humility of imperfection. Not to say that you must now bask in this notion of trying to remain imperfect, because that philosophy would be a disaster, especially in our professional lives where the intent is to always strive for perfection. Romans 9:16 says it's not of he that willeth neither of him that runneth but of God that sheweth mercy. By grace we can run the race and by his grace we will win the race, it is completely in the hands of God to crown our efforts. Do not give up nor condemn yourself for the lord has not condemned us.1 John 3:20. May the Grace of our Lord Jesus Christ be with you until the end.

ALLSTARS
A CHURCH WITHOUT WALLS
Salvation247.com

www.ingramcontent.com/pod-product-compliance
Lightning Source LLC
Chambersburg PA
CBHW031257130726
47988CB00008B/3395